I Know Why The Gay Man Dances

Joel Sadler-Puckering

Contents

- Foreword

- I Know Why the Gay Man Dances
- Rogue
- Extraordinary
- Welcome to Dystopia
- Underbelly
- Hen Night
- Ring Road
- Mancunian Dreams
- Queer
- Spice Up Your Life
- Dear Beyoncé
- Megastar
- #BrokenBritian
- Clown Republic
- The Ballad of Joyce Carol Vincent
- Ace
- King
- Queen
- Hummus
- How to Kill Their Dreams
- Line Them Up
- Cross Examination
- Statues
- Free Range Stupid
- Submission
- Eight of Diamonds
- Me and Mr God Knows Who
- I Quit
- Invisible Revolution
- Looting
- A Good Time to Leave the Country
- Year of The Giraffe

- Spring Is Now Here
- Riding Free
- Riding Free (Pt 2)
- Vows

Foreword

As an avid people watcher, I once stood and surveyed the gay bar I was in and watched man and boy alike.

They danced.

All of them: the old, the young, the fat, the thin, the ones with rhythm, the ones without and everyone in between.

All of them danced.

I pondered on the popular stereotype realizing itself before my eyes and in that moment, had to admit some truth in it.

For I while, I wondered why they danced.

Now, I think I know.

I Know Why the Gay Man Dances.

I know because I too have danced. Maya Angelou spoke about the caged bird and its song of freedom. The gay man dances for the exact same reason that the caged bird sings. For freedom.

This dance is not exclusive to the gay community. In the modern world, we are all caught up in a perpetual dance for freedoms that can be hard won and easily lost. Our dance should be one that weaves in and out of the unequal structures in society, challenging those that seek to seize control. It should be a dance of resistance and a dance of revolution.

This collection of poetry is about what happens when the spirit of freedom is taken from us. It is not just a gay experience; it is an experience shared by many subordinated groups.

These poems will take you on both a personal and political journey to explore the many ways that we, as human beings, might find our freedom compromised in modern life. How does it happen? Why does it happen? And perhaps most importantly, how can we try to understand and overcome it when it does happen?

I Know Why the Gay Man Dances

The man works hard and prays all day,
he feeds himself, has bills to pay.
The man works hard to build a life
and a house for his children and his wife.
He feels comfortable in the world he has made,
the beliefs he has held and foundations he's laid.
For the man feels accepted and recognised
and the man has freedom in his eyes.

But the gay man walks alone
and builds himself an empty home.
Alive.
but on the outside.
He thinks of the past and wasted chances.
His feet are tied
but he dances.

The gay man dances
for twisted love and cold romances.
The cage bird sings its freedom song
and the gay man dances so he belongs.

So dance.

Dance for love, dance for heartbreak.
Dance and show the world you're awake.
Dance for your mother, dance for her child.
Dance for the memory of Oscar Wild.
Dance in the face of those who don't listen.

Dance for the gay men who were thrown into prison.
Dance for the people who beat you and bash you.
Dance for the life of Justin Fashanu.
Dance in the sunlight, dance in the dark.
Dance for the vigil in Sackville Park.
Dance for the people whose minds are not ready.
Dance for Elton; dance for Freddy.
Dance for the invisible and those who know fear
And for every time you hear 'faggot' or 'queer'.

So dance.

Dance for the living.
Dance cos you can.

Dance for the freedom of every gay man.

Ever wonder why gay culture is often centres around the worship of movie stars and pop stars that marketed to us under the moniker 'gay icons'? I've taken the liberty of rewriting the rap in Madonna's 'vogue' and replacing the names with a few LGBT people that have had an impact on their own history:

Rogue

Elton John and Mckellen
Angie Zapta and girls like Ellen
Dennis Rodman, Gareth Thomas
Sometimes rights are taken from us

Lily Savage, Alan Turing
Straight gay icons feel so boring
Wilfred Owen, Oscar Wild
Carol Ann Duffy, write with style

They had grace, they had pride
Men like Michael Causer died
Alexander, Justin, Freddie, too
Harvey Milk: we remember you

Ladies with a point to make
Fellas dealing with self-hate
Don't just stand there, let's get to it
Be a rogue, there's nothing to it

Rogue (Rogue. Rogue.)

Extraordinary
(for Caster Semenya)

At 19 years old
You dazzled
Your physical prowess
Caught our attention
Talented. Extraordinary.

Then they looked
and noticed...

You were different.

Not curved enough
Not soft enough
Not woman enough
Jaw too defined
Muscles too defined
Too quick
Too black
Too strong
Shining too bright.

You were extraordinary.

They wanted you to be
Ordinary.

Like Turning before you
Legally binding and unapologetic
They suppressed you with chemicals
To make you blend in
with those more ordinary
Than yourself.

Undeterred, you came again.
Leading.
Baring the flag of
New found democracy.

Talented. Extraordinary.
Quick. Strong. Black.
Gold. Woman.

Welcome to Dystopia

We stare wide-eyed
and hypnotized
hysterical in our quest
for material satisfaction.

Megalomaniac millionaires
Seize absolute control
Using horror movie slogans
and deeply decisive division.

Misogynists far and wide
Step out of their cloaked disguises
And gloriously grab pussies
In euphoric masculine celebration

as the masses worship the plastic-fantastic,
half-naked, post human bodies
On MTV. They seductively trill
powerless sexual innuendo, distracting us

from foreign landscapes that explode
Faintly in the distance like a whisper.
We admire the view and don't notice
children washed up on our beaches.

Underbelly

Where the ruthless
And the toothless
Fornicate
To dance Music

Where the lonely
And the soul-less
Purposely
Loose control
Of themselves

Where the oversexed
And the under-blessed
Put their pride aside
And puff out their chest

Where base minds go
To fester or grow
And cling to the edge
Of a cultural hole

Where liquor is cheap
And grown men weep
Masters of nothing
Versed in self-deceit

Where the party is done
And the embarrassed sun
Sucks the vigour
From the plastic fun

Where the superficial
Do not survive
Where ugly and the honest

Thrive
Where the crazies drive
Until they arrive

At The Underbelly

Carrying their hearts
In an Aldi bag

Hen Night

Expectations are up as the glitter comes down
Thick glossy make up paints over a frown
A pink, fluffy garter, tiara or crown
Army of eye lashes – the girls on the town.

Clattering heels on the cold concrete cobbles
The one with the blisters, moving just at a hobble
An echoing holler *'give your head a wobble'*
An angry reply leads to cat-fight or squabble.

Destination Canal Street, the hens make a splash
as they hit Via Fossa with oodles of cash
heading to the bar with an elbowing dash,
a pair of high heels and a 'bride to be' sash.

A star of the night in a tight fitting dress
thinks *'it's a waste'* 'cos the guys aren't impressed
Her mate round the corner, wound up in a mess
vomit on her tits and hair stuck to her head.

The end of the night - straight to Safads for food
some pushing and shoving: the punters are rude.
'Be as quick as we can', the gaggle conclude
cos the bride is outside and divorcing her shoes.

Ring Road

M60. Commuting.
One of thousands on
Endless grey Tarmac
Stretching out
To nowhere
And everywhere.

Commercial radio hums
The same old tune
On rotation.
Hollow blue eyed ballads
And empty baseless dance tracks
Vibrate lazily against
The car window.

Grey melancholic humdrum
Descends and coats
the edge of the city
as the silhouette
Of The Hilton Tower
Fades in distance
Along with dreams
Of exotic beaches
And Summer holidays
We thought would never end.

Mancunian Dreams

Manchester.
Dickensian coke town.
Laugh in the face of pain.
Joke town.

Looming factories built on
slave trade profits
Now home to rainbow races
That mingle
With relative ease.

Hedonistic nights
With psychedelic musical landscapes
That stretch far beyond us
And reinvent us
Like Turing invented his computer
And punish us
Like a deadly bite
From a cyanide apple

Mondays that range from
Blue to Happy
Tuesdays offering hope
That floats down
The Rochdale Canal
With all the optimism
Of a drowning shopping trolley.

We know 'the Hacienda must be built'
So we build it
with the dream
that if you live in Manchester,
you will always be able to dance.

Queer

Speckled sea of light
Twists around the night
An empty soul
Out of control
Bodies out of sight

Solid red brickwork
Built out of all our hurt
Hearts alone
On a mobile phones
As empty voices lurk

Echoed muted roars
Reflecting all your flaws
Don't know the cost
But we all feel lost
Virgins turn to whores

We slowly flit about
Hairstyles full of doubt
No rainbows arc
Here in the dark
Our inner lights put out

An Empty glass of wine
Long White powder line
So we stay here
Because we feel queer
And everything feels fine

Spice Up Your Life

The homeless in Manchester
Stand still and lifeless
High on Spice or Angel Dust
Next to post-boxes
Painted gold to honour
Olympic athletes.

The public panic but walk by
blithely until they get home
where they describe what they
saw on public forums with an
apparent discerning tone:

'Wrapped around a barrier at
Piccadilly Station'

'Must be horrific beyond imagination'

'Completely abandoned
Symptom of neglect'

'Fitting, foaming
Stiff eyes rolling'

'No one helps each other'

'Never seen it so bad'

'We won't be returning anytime soon'

Dear Beyonce – I Woke Up Like *THIS*
I woke up like
A corpse
Snatched from a grave
In the middle of its
Oblivious death.
I woke up groggily and sluggishly
Heavy headed
And forced myself to sit up
Come round
And breath.
I woke up with hair stuck on end
Neck contorted
Face crumpled
Feeling every one of my 35 years
Ache in my lower back.
I woke up reluctantly
But with tenacity
I placed both feet on the cluttered carpet
Ready to face the day's ritual
Face my public.
Ready to smile
Make niceties
And say
'Good morning'

And then there was you.
Shining and shimmering
Broadcasting into their heads
Across electronic beams
Plastic perfection,
You cry
'I woke up like this'

Meanwhile, I woke up a mess
And I woke up to you

Megastar

Flash of a camera, a glamorous thought,
Strutting around in a gown that she bought
The face of her mother, clearly distraught
Body laid bare, a post-mortem report

Lonely hotel room, a half-eaten snack
Open Champaign, an empty blister pack
Portable mirror, white crystal of crack
Ninety three degrees, an almost boiling bath

Repeated prescription for when she's feeling rough
And an ash tray filled full of used cigarette butts
Perforated septum, abrasions and cuts
A black adult female found face down in the tub

No hair, dignity and without an apology
Megastar victim of her own sociology
We reflect on her death with half-baked psychology
As right-winged newspapers print a full toxicology

Her eyebrows were sparse, she had mild emphysema
With tumours on her uterus and pulmonary edema
A congested colon
broken body diva
Yet so many women once wished they could be her

#BrokenBritain

A country torn to pieces, full to the brim with sin
A state that fills us full of hate until it eats us from within
Protecting our elections so that public school boys win
It chokes the growth, ensuring revolution can't begin

Thought control and mind control by unelected press
Multinational capitalists are charging more for less
Penny pinching scrimping causes working people stress
An education system where postcodes decide success

Desperate, defensive folk elect the BNP
Young men think it nobel when they contract an STD
Ministers that masquerade and tell us thought is free
Blaming poverty on immigrants, spreading hate through our TV

Battle lines divide us so that we denounce the youth
Conspiracy to blame the poor; a fabricated truth
Claims of criminality without a shred of proof
Misplaced sense of righteousness, shouted from the roof

Transgender offender writing in The Daily Mail
Examination politics causes council kids to fail
Searching for a bargain whilst our souls for sale
The level of illiteracy that flourishes in jail

Lonely in the margin, we're confounded by division
Uneducated ministers take educational decision
Using propaganda to lock us in a mental prison
We reduce ourselves to hashtags cos we live in #BrokenBritain

Clown Republic

Clowns on the corner
Counterfeit make-up
Clowns in the commons
Brexit and shake up

Clowns see your car
And jump right upon on it
Clowns on TV
With a racist rhetoric

Clowns in the shadows
Brandish a knife
Clowns behind closed doors
Controlling your life

Clowns look for meaning
And dress up for fun
Clowns support Trump
So that they keep their gun

Clowns in our cities
Our streets and our shires
Clowns at the top
With their selfish desires

Clowns are increasing
And this shit's not funny
Clowns, banks and businesses
Stealing our money

Clowns in the papers
Fear in our hearts
Lives that are over
Before they can start

The Ballad of Joyce Carol Vincent
(The story of isolation at the heart of our nation)

Has anybody seen my old friend Joyce?
I've not seen her for some time
I forgot to call or text or write
But I'm sure that she'll be fine

A party girl in a tight blue dress
She would always make heads turn
Eyes so full of life – A star of the night
For acceptance she did yearn

Singing in a booth with a dream of fame
And to be one day recognized
Seen on video tape at a Mandela speech
Clapping words she viewed as wise

And like all of us, she dreamed of love
But to her, it wasn't kind
Men longed for and to devour her
Violent rejection she did find

Has anybody seen my old friend Joyce?
I've not seen her for some time
I forgot to call or text or write
But I'm sure that she'll be fine

Above the shopping centre
In bleak Wood Green
Is where Joyce waited for us all
Christmas presents wrapped
And the TV on
post piled high in the hall

And as years passed by, she waited there
Till debt collectors did break in
They found her rotting corpse
with a shopping bag
Bank manager: next of kin.

The neighbours noticed a rotten smell
But urban hearts are unforgiving
They also heard her TV on
And assumed it a sign of living

Has anybody seen my old friend Joyce?
I've not seen her for some time
I forgot to call or text or write
But I'm sure that she'll be fine

Ace

Ace enters his local haunt
Surveys the room
To search for
The next lucky girl
To experience the
Full force of his uber-charm.

Ace. Stud. Prowler.

Virile vagina warrior.
On the charm offensive.
Tight T-Shirt.
Guns out.
Argos Chain.
Sunday league.
Hall of fame.

Intentions as empty
And words as fake
As the hollow,
plastic darts trophy
That takes pride of place
On his masculine mantel.

Ace. Winner. Charmer.

The topic of many
Kiss and tell stories told

Left his girl
For another fool
His baby less than one month old.

Queen

Candy-floss haired
Matriarch
A bite in your bark

A monkey-nut-footed
Cart horse Trekking
Towards concrete factories
Producing
Yesterday's news
But you never choose
To sing the blues

Always funny
Claiming
'The real poor don't
Ask you for money
Because deep inside
they value their pride.'

An Acid tongue
Made Strong
From general lashings
And daily ear bashings

Out of fashion
Hair like michael Jackson
Prone to overreaction
And lyrical waxing

About everything from
An orphaned youth
To eccentric relatives
And ugly neighbors
Spoiling your view

Ice-cold winters
At the end your reign
Standing strong
When your son was gone
Leading your family

Trekking on

You were never the same
Body and spirt broken
And when that final winter came
You passed on your crown
On Boxing Day
To those who knew your pain

King

Real Aleing
Life plain sailing
Priorities failing
Off spring need saving

But a king does
Not have the inclination
To get involved
He's Too busy losing
Control

Getting his fill
Of the good life
Practicing his skill
In golf
And shot drinking

And football chanting
And petty conversation
That may save the nation
But don't put your faith in

The King

The king of disappointment
Of absence
Of straightforward
Uncompromising
Self obsession
With no expression
More brutal than violence

It's an empty reign
Plagued by
Emotional silence

Hummus

'I can't believe you've never tried hummus'
I recall a friendly but bland
college mate exclaim,
handing me a roll covered in it
as we made our way to
look around Bristol University.

I was 18 and this was all new.

My working class pallet
could tell the difference between
Asda Smart Price fish fingers
And Captain Birdseye.
I also knew the seismic differences
between garden peas and marrow fat.
But not much more.

Many years later, I pushed
my trolley around Tesco Didsbury,
angry that the hummus
and dips section had moved:
I stopped.
I wondered what my 18 year old
self would think of his
Hummus munching
Middle class counterpart.

How to Kill Their Dreams

Take one Standard English education
Apply public school ideologies
Separate George, Lennie, Atticus
and dispose of anything else American.
Add a liberal helping of
White male authors.
Remove creativity.
Shift a grade boundary here and there,
Sieve out marks
for speaking and listening
And test them until thoroughly baked.
Once cooked through,
fully disillusioned and failed,
Serve them on a plate
To capitalist organizations
Who will devour them whole
and keep them working
In minimum wage jobs
Until their dreams are fully
dead.

Line Them Up

I watched them in rows
Table behind table
The gifted
The talented
The slightly less able
The scholars
The Scallies
The mainstream
And the misfits
The higher
The foundation
The failures
And the resits
The sighs
Rolling eyes
And the unclassified
The wise
Telling lies
The successful surprise
The ridiculous
The sublime
The C-D borderline

All in line
When we die
Looming clock
Counting time

Cross Examination

Sea of sepia.
Coffee sipping
and hair splitting
over upper and lower case
eyes.

Disagreements and sighs.

Standard English conversation
about what
success should entail
and what kind of communication
should fail.

Qualifications bought
and sold.
Guidelines told
so that public schools
retain control.

I deliberate
over what's more tragic:
the literary magic
of a bullet piercing
Lennie's head;
or Romeo and Juliet
when they're dead;

Or is it Jimmy Smith
who wrote two pages
about getting a 'nice house'
and a 'good job'.

Two pages.
One full stop.

Statues

Robot rodents
Rat race frozen
Slow down time
Open minds closing

Truth one sided
Grey scale blinded
Schools for fools
And the undecided

Heavy and weighted
Till we're suffocated
Don't try to climb
Grounded by self-hatred

Status quo protection
Void of self-reflection
We wait in vain
For a resurrection

Stopped in motion
Overlooking commotion
Frozen still
Trying to fix what's broken

Free Range Stupid

Sometimes I want to slap you
around your stupid face
Because you couldn't organize
And orgy in a brothel
Watching your spineless attempts
To inspire the disaffected youth
Is like watching a wanton boy
Poke a wasp's nest with a flimsy stick
I'm infuriated by your stupid ideas
And frustrated by your lack of conviction
Your expectations are so low
That they dip beneath the sanity line
The way you talk about 'these kids'
Is an insult to anyone
That ever lived in a council house
I've watched you squirm like a worm
And use undignified and debased
excuses for your utter incompetence
I've watched you hurry round and
Cover shit up to hide your failings
Enough is enough of your
stupid stupid shit.
You stand oblivious in opposition
To everything I've ever stood for
You are ruining lives and creating
A home for the free range stupid.

Submission

We sip Vodka
From tin cups
As if we are in
Cold War Russia

We pay 7 pound 95
For the privilege

Held to ransom
By a weakening pound

We do nothing
And wait for revolution

But nothing happens.

Eight of Diamonds

He stood at the bar
Reflective
And surveyed the room.

It was like little pieces
Of his soul had shattered
And were everywhere.

His older self at the bar
Watching from the outside
Alone and shunned judgmentally
By his teenage self
In fashionably drastic clothes
And a stiff, uptight haircut.

Across from them, his rebellious self
Hypnotized by narcotics
Barely recognizable
trapped in the moment
And tangled in the beat of the song
Not noticing his lustful self
Making eyes at boys hoping they
noticed his inner beauty
And tried to devour it.

On the table nearby, his in love self
Stared longingly and expectantly
Into the eyes of the man opposite
Expectant and full of hope
As his out of love self stood quietly,
almost disappearing into the crowd
Looking down disappointedly
At his phone reading a

hurtful text message that
Felt so dangerous it wounded him.

The whole scene was interrupted
Suddenly and abruptly
By his violent self. Consumed
By rage and blinded by
An unknown and undignified
Red mist and startling everyone else,
Making them withdraw from
Their moments and stare in fear.

Then in the mirror,
Looking calmly back
Was his current self.
Experiencing one moment of clarity.
Still. Surrounded by shadows
Of his past and his future.
Each one shining and unique
in the moment
And completely unaware
Of what is to come.

Me and Mr God Knows Who...

What kind of fuckery is this?
You made me miss the Sweedish pop star Robyn gig
- the one she cancelled
and By the time it was rearranged
You and I were estranged

You were 19 when we met
And sleeping on your ex's floor
Now I can hear you snore
On the other side of the door
And I'm the ex
And It's my floor

I'm sorry that I cheated on you
With Mr God Knows Who
But did you really expect
It to be acceptable
To not fuck me for two years
On the off chance
My first boyfriend had HIV?

I needed to know
If I was actually attractive
And not universally detested

I bet you never did get tested

Anyway: whatever.
Serves me right for believing
A 19 year old when they said they'd
Love me forever

I Quit

Today: I quit.
Because I no longer believed
In what I was seeing.
And feeling...

Presented
with a situation that
Brought back the horrors
Of past disillusionments
Of a system that
Does not work for us all.

So I followed the advice
Of a hundred Facebook memes
And I quit.

I quit to find something
I can believe in.

I quit because
Sometimes
Shit just is not right.

Invisible Revolution

The Revolution will not be
Printed on T-Shirts and sold
For twenty quid by multi-national
Corporations that pay no tax.

The Revolution will not be
Recorded into perfect pop song
And sold on iTunes by Sony music
Making three or four white men rich .

The Revolution will not be
Diluted and turned into bite size
Memes and Soundbites that we can tune in
And out over petty lunchtime conversations.

The Revolution will not be
Broadcast between shrewd advertising
And framed within accessible narratives
That reduce the people to their essence.

The Revolution must take root in us
shaping our words and our actions.

The Revolution must become us.

Looting

Hood man, run man, Plasma TV
Loot that, shoot that, everything is free
Sweat shops working for less than ten pee
Brand it, package it, selling it to me.

Smash it, burn it, fire in the sky
Posters billboards, catching my eye
Riding, looting, BMX bike
MP, expenses, another new lie

Adidas, Henley's, Nike Air Max
Boots and Top Man, off shore tax
Transparent windows, a shattered crack
Sirens blaring; the youth attack

Dark conglomerates, rich and poor
Retail therapy, label whore
Shopping precinct, kick down the door
Whatever we have, we still want more.

A Good Time to Leave the Country

Homophobic B&B
Wispas that cost you 55p
Nothing ever comes for free
It's a good time to leave the country.

Gun men stalk the country-side,
Knife crime, vandals, homicide,
Dark desires televised
guilty,
If the press decide.

Wages freezing, taxes rising,
Careful what we're televising,
Eating, drinking, supersizing
Heavy hearts are not surprising

People try to look attractive
Highly strung on tight elastic
Megastars that look fantastic
Everybody made of plastic.

Jager Bombs and mass confusion
Trying to promote illusion
Boozing choosing your delusion.
Working hard to keep refusing.

Inclusion minister goes hysterical
And tries to save the homosexuals
masquerades as intellectual
making laws like she's protecting you

August brings a summer shower.
For every sweet you get a sour
Globalisation exerts power

It casts a shadow like the Hilton tower

so
Stop, pause, recollect
Aretha Franklin wants respect
We all need some time to reflect
and feel the summer's full effect

So now you know, the past is done
It's time to stop and have some fun.
In California, in the sun
We hope 'A Change Gonna Come'.

We've had enough so
Let's go
Let's go
Have a ball and have a disco.

Leave the country
Pronto
pronto
Make your way to San Francisco.

Spring is Now Here

Frost this morning
grog in my head
Took some resolve
to get my ass out of bed

My past made me heavy
nearly took me to black
Temperatures stayed low
weighing down on my back

But this evening feels fresh
There's a warmth on my skin
And it feels like a new chance
For me can begin

I see warm April colours
In front on my eyes
And things that once happened to me
Made me wise

It took a long time to come
But I no longer know fear
I have stopped and exhaled
Because Spring is now here

Year of The Giraffe

May we stand tall above this mess
Surveying the world
From a great height
Not lowering our heads
But raising them
In elegant defiance
And thoughtful indignation

May we be fabulous
In our animal print
Rainbow colours
Rubbing noses as we go
Knowing that love
Has no boundaries
Even for multi-coloured mammals
Like us

May we contrast vividly
To the darkness of our environments
Look them square in the eyes
With absolutely no shame
In our difference
And simply whisper

We. Are. Beautiful.

Riding Free

Without direction
I carried on
Free
From the burden
Of the little man
On my back
Trying to assert control

I galloped on
Amongst the others
who were coated in
Glorious colours
That when united
Made a rainbow of hope

And then there were those
Burdened by the
Weight of expectation
Falling and trampled
And left for dead
In the ditch

And there I was
Dark and colourless
Alone in this race
But free
Focused
Determined
To finish on my own terms

Riding Free (Pt 2)

Into the distance
We drive
Away from humdrum
Until we arrive
At a place where
Laughter lives
Away from
The clutches
Of capitalism
And into the arms
Of hedonism
We run like
The bastard child
Of Candi Staton
And Nile Rogers
We disappear
Delighted into
The light
The sky is vast
And stretched out
In front of us
Possibilities of transcendence
Are at our fingertips

Vows

I used to think that
love was sacrificing
All you are
And all that you have
For another
That it was about
Being consumed
And losing yourself
Completely.

Then there was you...

Beautiful you.
You have taught me
That love is
Simple and honest
And open and uplifting.
It is the strength
To be the best version
Of yourself.

It is nurturing and hopeful
It is being together
and growing together
And becoming part of each other

On this day, in front of
Our friends and family,
I promise you this:

I will always
try my best to make you happy
I will always
Be silly and laugh with you

I will always
Make statues on escalators with you
I will always
Help you to build your dreams

And finally,
In the words of
Whitney Houston:
I will always love you.

Printed in Great Britain
by Amazon